GREEK ATHLETICS

David Buchanan

Douglas Ewart High School, Newton Stewart

LONGMAN

1 : NOW AND THEN

The modern Olympic Games are organised on a huge scale. Some 8,000 young men and women from all over the world compete every four years in 21 different sports for medals and glory.

The ancient Greek Games were on a much smaller scale. There were only a few hundred competitors, and only four sports: athletics, boxing, wrestling and chariot racing. In athletics there were only eight events compared with nearly 40 now, and the total events were about 20 compared with nearly 200.

But the main difference is that the modern Olympics involve over 130 nations—the Greek Games were only for the peoples of Greece.

This is the Olympic Stadium at Munich in West Germany, where the 1972 Games were held

Athletics were popular all over Greece and continued over many years. The original Olympic Games, held at Olympia, lasted over a thousand years, from 776 BC to 396 AD. At first, only a few cities took part with competitors coming from the Greek colonies as well as from the mainland of Greece. Athletes came from the Greek islands, Asia Minor, Cyrene in North Africa, Sicily and Italy.

The top sporting cities taking part in the games at Olympia in this period (from 776 BC to about 300 BC) were Sparta with 46 victories, Elis (the local area round Olympia) with 30, Athens with 22, and Croton in Italy with 21.

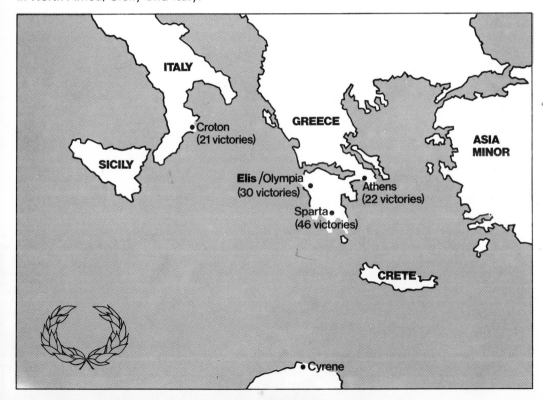

Map showing where Greek Athletes came from, and which were the top sporting cities (766–300 BC)

From 300 BC on, as athletics became more and more popular, athletes came to Greece from a much wider area. In the second century BC Greece was conquered by Rome and became a part of the Roman Empire. This probably helped to spread Greek athletics even further.

We know that over a hundred cities held athletics contests. You can see some of them on the map. Even Naples and Rome itself staged games, but athletics never really caught on in the western Roman Empire—they preferred gladiators and chariot races.

The top city (at Olympia) in this period was Alexandria in Egypt with 43 victories, second was the island of Rhodes with 19 and Elis was third with 17. Athens and Sparta, which by this time were rather unimportant places, fell off badly with only nine victories between them.

Map showing the cities that took part in the Olympic games (300 BC onwards)

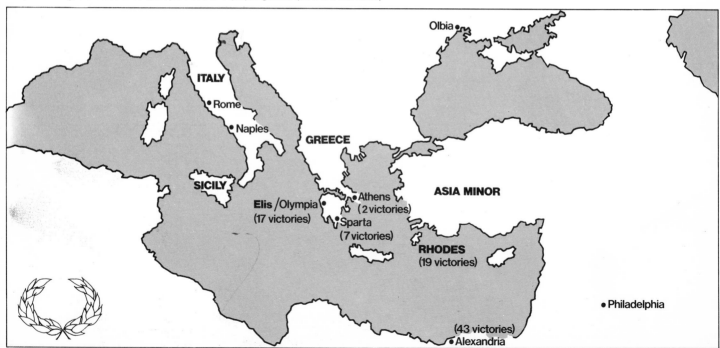

We get our knowledge of Greek athletics in four different ways:

1 There are a number of stadiums which have been excavated.
2 We have stories of athletes and famous contests. There are very few books telling us such things as the rules of each contest, or how you entered.
3 We have lists of victors at Olympia and elsewhere for most years.
4 Finally, we have vase paintings and sculptures which sometimes hinder rather than help. For example, look at the painting on this page, where the artist has drawn the runners with the left arm and left foot forward at the same time. It is almost impossible to run this way— try it yourself!

You can see the problems if you imagine someone in 2,000 years' time, trying to work out how football was played in the 1970s with nothing to go on but the ruins of Wembley Stadium, a list of F.A. Cup winners, some old photographs and a few stories about Bobby Charlton!

Runners (from a vase painting)

The Crown Games

The Games held at Olympia (they should really be called the 'Olympian' Games) were the most important Games in Greece for over a thousand years, and Olympic champions were most famous.

But the Olympic Games were only one of four **Crown Games**, which were most widely known. (These were so called because they awarded crowns or wreaths to the winners.) The other three were the Pythian Games at Delphi, the Isthmian Games at Corinth, and the Nemean Games at Nemea.

The Olympic and Pythian Games were held every four years, and the Isthmian and Nemean Games every two years. The Olympic and Nemean Games were in honour of Zeus, the King of the Gods, the Pythian Games were in honour of Apollo, the God of music and athletics, and the Isthmian Games were in honour of Poseidon, the God of the sea.

While the games were being held, the Greeks observed a **sacred truce**. This meant that athletes could compete safely at these places, even if the cities they came from were at war with one another.

Map showing the four cities which staged the Crown Games

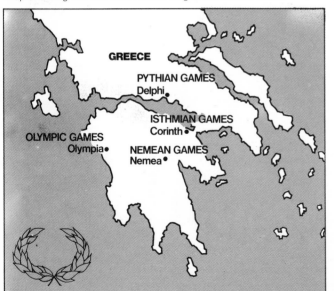

The tracks were often left uncared-for between competitions. Here you can see an athlete clearing a track of stones

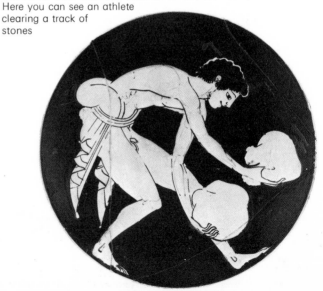

Prizes

Many different sorts of prizes were awarded to the winners at the Games. The Crown Games awarded different kinds of wreaths—wild olive at Olympia, laurel at Delphi, pine leaves at Corinth, and wild celery at Nemea. Elsewhere the winners got more valuable prizes, often shields or cups. Winners at Pellene in Asia Minor received warm leather jerkins, and Athens offered pitchers of oil.

An important difference between the modern Olympics and the Greek Games was that the competitors then were not amateurs, as they must be nowadays. Athens, for example, offered good money prizes to athletes who did well in competitions in other cities. The victorious athletes got a civic reception when they returned home, a large money award, and often a pension for life. Writers were hired to compose special victory poems in their honour; Pindar of Thebes became famous for this.

A relief showing the prizes won by a victorious Athenian athlete. From left to right they are: a pitcher from Athens, a wreath from Corinth, a shield from Argos, and a wreath from Nemea. (Taken from the base of a statue.)

Professional athletes became more and more common in the later period of the Greek Games. Athletes even had their own trades unions, which fought very hard for their members' conditions of work. They organised their own meetings, and offered money prizes. In the first century BC athletes did not have to do military service or pay taxes!

Here is the prize list from Aphrodisias, a small town in Asia Minor, in the first century AD.

Short Sprint (about 200 metres)	1250 denarii
Double Sprint (about 400 metres)	1000 denarii
Long Distance Race (length unknown)	750 denarii
Armour Race	500 denarii
Pentathlon (long jump, discus, javelin, sprint and wrestling)	500 denarii
Boxing	2000 denarii
Wrestling	2000 denarii
Pankration (all-in wrestling)	3000 denarii

(1000 denarii = £400)

Here you can see an athlete's triumphant return to his home town. He is on the horse, and you can see, from left to right, the crowd, a flute-player, an entertainer, a workman clearing the street, and a spectator trying to get a better view

QUESTIONS

1 How many sports were there in the ancient Games? (page 2)
2 Name 3 differences between the modern and ancient Games. (page 2)
3 What is the main difference? (page 2)
4 How long did the ancient Olympics last? (page 3)
5 What were the two top sporting cities which competed at Olympia? (pages 3 and 4)
6 Why were athletics not so popular in Roman times? (page 4)
7 From what four sources do we get our knowledge of Greek athletics? (page 5)
8 What was the 'sacred truce'? (page 6)
9 Name the four Crown Games. Where were they each held? (page 6)
10 What prizes were won at the Crown Games? (page 7)

THINGS TO DO

1 Imagine you are attending an Olympic athlete's triumphant return to his own city. Describe the scene, then draw a picture of it.
2 Find out all you can about the latest Olympics— nations competing, number of competitors, sports, athletic events, total events—and make a table comparing this with the ancient Olympics.
3 What is the difference between amateur and professional sport? Do you think it is better for major sporting events such as the Olympic games to be for amateurs or professionals? What did the Greeks think about this? Get your teacher to help you to organise a class debate.
4 Look at the prize-list from Aphrodisias on page eight. What sports have the most prize money? Why do you think this is so? Find out which modern sports have the most prize money and say why you think some sports carry more than others.

2 : STADIUMS

Olympia

Olympia is in the province of Elis, in the south west of Greece, in the fertile valley of the river Alpheus. The buildings of the sports stadium are in a very ruined state, and if you went there you might be rather disappointed. But a hundred years ago, you could not even see any ruins; the whole site was buried under ten feet of mud from the river. It was excavated by a German archaeologist called Dorpfeld.

And yet we know a great deal about the buildings at Olympia. We even know, in great detail, about some which have completely vanished. How is this possible? The answer is simple—**Pausanias**. He was a Greek from Asia Minor who visited Olympia in 174 AD and wrote down everything he saw. It is from his book *A Description of Greece* that we can give you exact details of what Olympia looked like.

Apart from the stadium and Hippodrome (used for chariot-racing), Olympia consisted of a sacred area called the **Altis** and a number of other buildings. Inside the Altis was the Temple of Zeus (king of the gods). The foundations of this temple can still be seen today. In the temple was the 12 metre high statue of Zeus, which was regarded as one of the Seven Wonders of the World.

This is all that is left of the entrance to the stadium at Olympia today

Below you can see an artist's impression of what the sacred area might have looked like. You can see the Temple of Zeus, the Temple of Hera, the queen of the gods, and beside that a line of Treasuries. These belonged to various Greek cities and were used to store and display offerings to Zeus. Notice also the Painted Colonnade (a covered walk with pillars), which was famous for its echo.

Other buildings included hostels for athletes and officials, practice areas and baths.

The stadium lay to the east of the Altis, and was reached by a vaulted passageway. The first feeling you would have, visiting it, is that it's nothing like a modern stadium.

The ancient track is a long rectangle, measuring 200 metres by 30. In longer races the runners had to turn 180° round a turning post.

A modern track such as the White City in London is oval, apart from one straight stretch used for short sprints. There are no sharp bends at all, and there is a large area of grass in the centre for non-running events.

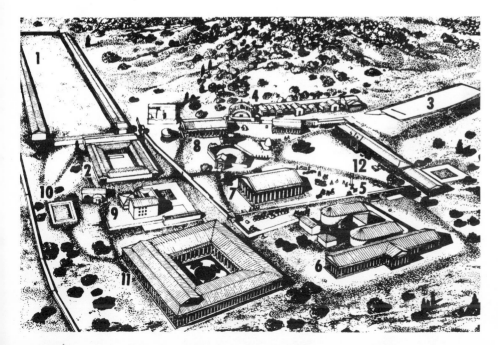

This is how Olympia looked in the second century A.D. **1** Gymnasium, **2** Palaestra, **3** Stadium, **4** Treasuries, **5** Statues of Olympic victors, **6** Council house, **7** Temple of Zeus, **8** Temple of Hera, **9** Indoor baths, **10** Swimming bath, **11** Hotel accommodation, **12** The Painted Colonnade.

Seating accommodation at Olympia was very poor. There was one small stand, probably for officials and special guests. But most of the spectators had to sit on the grass embankments. This is very different from a modern stadium, where spectators have comfortable seats and shelter from rain.

Olympia was, in fact, well known for its discomforts. A writer called Epiktetos gives us this picture in the second century AD:

Don't you get roasted by the sun at Olympia? Don't you get crushed by the crowds? Don't you find it impossible to get a bath? Don't you get soaked when it rains?

Don't you get an overdose of noise and irritation? Yet you steel your heart and put up with it because you think the spectacle makes it worthwhile.
Epiktetos 1.6.26

The stadium at Olympia as it is today

And yet the games at Olympia must have been an exciting and colourful five days. Apart from the contests, there would have been processions and ceremonies, mainly religious in nature.

The picture on this page shows a victory ceremony. The victor is on horseback, with a herald in front, who is announcing the details of the victory (notice the words falling from his mouth). Behind them is a man carrying his prize, a **tripod**, or three-legged stool.

A victory ceremony (from a vase painting). You can see the winner of a horse race riding in with a slave carrying his trophy

Olympia also drew the largest crowds, as it was the most important competition in Greece. People flocked to the stadium from all over the eastern Mediterranean, perhaps, in many cases, to see a local athlete compete. There was fierce rivalry, not just between the athletes, but between rival groups of supporters.

Dio Chrysostom, writing in the second century AD, describes the behaviour of the crowd at Alexandria thus:

When they enter the stadium, it is as if they were under the influence of drugs. They forget everything they have ever learned, and say and do the first thing that comes into their heads.

When you go inside, who could describe the bawling, the frenzy, the sudden changes of expression and colour on the faces, and the swearing?

What a difference there is when they're cheering their own men, and when they're insulting their rivals!
Dio Chrysostom 32.74 and 40·29

The sporting centre at Olympia also had hot and cold baths. These were very important to the athletes who paid great attention to personal cleanliness. Each one usually brought a flask of oil for massage, and a metal **strigil** or scraper to scrape off the oily mixture.

Cleanliness, of course, is always important in sports involving a lot of physical exertion, but it was especially important to Greek athletes, who performed completely naked. We do not know exactly why they did this, but certainly they did it without embarrassment.

In fact, the Greeks often boasted of their all-over tan, and contrasted it with the pale and sickly look of the Persians, who always wore clothes.

After the race: the athlete on the left is having his foot attended to by a slave, the one in the middle is pouring oil from a flask, and the one on the right is using a towel. On the opposite page you can see an athlete using a strigil

Delphi

The second most important sporting centre in Greece was **Delphi**, where the Pythian Games were held. Delphi was mainly known as the place where the Oracle of Apollo was. Apollo was the god of music, athletics and prophecy, which means telling the future. People came here from all over the world to consult the priests of Apollo about what the future might bring.

Delphi is situated on the slopes of Mount Parnassus, 115 miles west of Athens, overlooking the Gulf of Corinth. Today you can see the remains of the Castalian Spring, where pilgrims bathed, the Temple of Apollo, where they consulted the Oracle, the Theatre, and the Stadium.

Delphi complex showing **1** Gulf of Corinth, **2** the stadium, **3** the theatre, **4** the temple of Apollo, **5** the Castalian Spring

The stadium at Delphi is the best preserved and most famous in the world. The seats for the spectators along the northern and western sides are very well preserved; those to the south have crumbled away.

As is usual in Greek stadiums, one end (the western) is rounded, and one straight side (the northern) is slightly curved. Both these things enabled the spectators to see better.

At the eastern end are the foundations of a fine ornamental arch, and a well preserved starting-line. This has two grooves, which the runners stood on, to give them more spring at the start. They served the same purpose as modern starting-blocks.

The starting-line

QUESTIONS

1 How did Pausanias add to our knowledge of Olympia? (page 10)

2 Which of the Seven Wonders of the World could be found at Olympia? (page 10)

3 What are the main differences between the stadium at Olympia and a modern one? (page 11)

4 What sorts of discomforts did spectators have to suffer at Olympia according to Epiktetos? Why did people come despite these? (page 12)

5 What prize is the man in the vase painting on page 13 carrying? (page 13)

6 Why does Dio Chrysostom mention 'the sudden changes of expression and colour' in the face of the crowd? What do you think is happening? (page 14)

7 What was a *strigil* and how was it used? (page 14)

8 What, apart from athletics, was Delphi known for? (page 15)

9 What is remarkable about the stadium at Delphi? (page 16)

THINGS TO DO

1 Draw the ancient victory ceremony described on page 13.

2 Find out what cities the Olympic Games have been held in since 1945. On a map you have traced, show where they are. Then mark in Greece, and the places where the original Olympics were held. Use a different colour for the ancient cities.

3 What buildings, apart from the athletics stadium, are used in the modern Olympics? Which ones would you not expect to find in an ancient Greek sports centre? Make out two lists comparing the buildings of Ancient Greece with those of today.

4 Look at Dio Chrysostom's comments on crowds on page 14.
Discuss in class whether this applies to modern crowds or not.

5 How do you think the Oracle of Apollo at Delphi was able to tell the future? Find out all you can about it.

6 Find out what were the other six wonders of the ancient world. Make a list of all seven in your exercise books.

3 : EVENTS

Running

There were four races in the athletics programme:
the **stade** or short sprint (one length of the track)
the **diaulos** or double sprint (two lengths)
the race in armour (two lengths)
the **dolichos** or long-distance race (number of lengths
unknown: possibly ten).

The *stade* race took its name from the word 'stadium'
which is a Greek measurement of about 200 metres (and
also the name of the building where the games were held).
The man who won the *stade*, especially if he won at
Olympia, was thought of as the fastest man on earth.

Runners in the *diaulos* and *dolichos* had to go round a
turning-post at the far end of the track before their second
length; indeed the *dolichos* needed two turning-posts. You
can easily imagine the jostling that went on as the runners
went round the post. As you can see in the picture, there
was always an umpire there, armed with a stick, to punish
anyone who was tempted to swing round it.

The turning-post (from a vase painting)

The race in armour means what it says—the runners ran for two lengths with helmet and shield. It was not thought very important, and most people looked on it as a kind of egg-and-spoon race.

We don't know how the times of ancient runners compared with modern ones, as the Greeks had no stop-watches. But what really mattered then, as now, was who was the first past the finishing post.

Race in armour (from a vase painting)

The starting line in the sprints was originally a scratch in the sand. This was later replaced by stone blocks, which can still be seen in many stadiums. These had grooves cut in them for the runners to stand on while waiting for the start, rather like modern starting-blocks.

The stadium at Corinth has a strange starting device called a **husplex**. This was like the starting gates used in modern horse racing. Each runner stood behind a wooden arm which was moved up and down by the starter. As you can see in the photograph, the cords held by the starter have gradually worn away grooves in the stone.

Husplex at Corinth. In the foreground you can see the deep pit where the starter stood. The grooves made by the cords lead from it to the starting line where the wooden 'starting gates' were

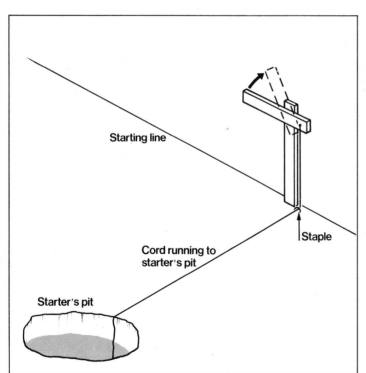

The Pentathlon

The pentathlon was made up of five events: long jump, discus, javelin, stade race, and wrestling. The first three were known as the **Triad** or 'Big Three'. Anyone who won the *Triad* was the outright winner, as three wins were needed for victory and the *Triad* was always run first. In this case, the other two events were not held.

But if no competitor won all three events of the *Triad*, then a *stade* race was run. If there was still no one with the three wins needed, then the wrestling was held. (Of course only the winners of the first three events took part in the last two)

Thus it was possible for a man to win the long jump and the discus and still fail to win the pentathlon. It was also possible for a man to come second in each of the first three events and to be eliminated immediately, because only the first place counted.

Two of the events of the *Triad* are shown here: the discus and the javelin. The things hanging at the top are weights used by long jumpers

The Long Jump

A strange feature of the long jump was that athletes used weights, one in each hand, to drive themselves further. These weights, called **halteres**, can be seen in the vase painting on this page; they look like flat-irons, or sometimes telephone receivers.

Exactly how they were used is difficult to say. One idea is that they were swung from a standing position. But most people think that it was a *running* jump, as it is today. The weights must have been even more difficult to use in a running jump.

A jumper in mid-air swinging his weights forward. Notice the umpire again, using his stick

Bob Beamon, the holder of the world long jump record, from America

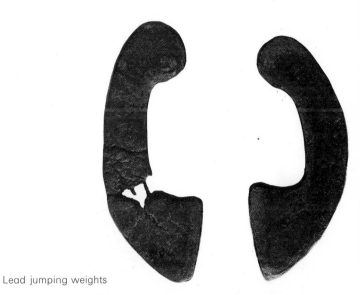

Lead jumping weights

The most famous jumper of the ancient world was **Phayllos** (pronounced fa-illos), who came from the Italian city of Croton. He is recorded as having jumped the amazing distance of nearly 17 metres—amazing because the present world record is 8·90 metres!

The Greek long jump was almost certainly a double or triple jump. The current world record for the triple jump, formerly known as the hop, step and jump, is 17·40 metres. If Phayllos' jump was a triple, then he was an outstanding athlete; if it was a double jump, then Phayllos must have been a superman.

In this passage taken from a modern book about Greek Athletics, you can read about how long jumpers were trained to the accompaniment of musical instruments.

A standing long jump had to be made from lines at the end of the sand-pit. As each of the trainees landed, a line was scored on the sand where his feet touched, and the instructor measured the distance covered with his rod. Faults in style were indicated, with a touch of the rod to emphasise them.

'Now,' the instructor told them, 'you can do the jump properly with the *halteres*.'

Grasping a pair of jumping-weights, an advanced student gave a demonstration of their use while the class watched intently.

'Remember this,' the instructor warned them, 'the jump doesn't count unless your footprints are regular. If you land one foot before the other, or if you fall or so much as stumble, then it's a false jump, and we won't even trouble to find out how far you've gone. The important thing isn't to cover the ground, but to show correct style.'

This vase painting shows an instructor at work. You can see, from left to right, a long jumper holding jumping weights, a javelin thrower, and a discus thrower.

But there were no false jumps in the demonstration. Grasping a weight in either hand, the student nodded to the flute-player. As the musical notes thrilled out, he swung the weights headhigh before him; paused, swung them forcibly downwards and bent slightly; paused when his hands were just under his knees, and swung his weights forward. Again he swung them backwards and then again forwards and then backwards once more.

But now, on the forward swing, by vigorously straightening his body and knees, he launched himself into the air. He swung legs and arms forward ready to land; but at the last moment he again swung his arms backwards; and the swing back, as the heavy jumping-weights went behind him, thrust him on, increasing the length of his jump. The class broke into a hum of appreciation as he made the perfect landing, and even the instructor gave him a grudging word of praise.

Olympic Runner — M. I. Evans

A long jumper practising to the music of the flute

The Discus

The second event in the *Triad* was throwing the discus, a large flat circular disc of metal or stone; discuses found so far weigh between six and nine kilos. The discus seems to have been thrown in roughly the same way as it is today; writers often describe the throw as a 'whirling round'.

Phayllos of Croton's performance with the discus is also recorded. The actual words are:

'He jumped 17 metres, but threw the discus 27 metres.'

A Greek sculptor called Myron made a statue of a discus thrower which is very famous. It shows the thrower at the top of the backward swing, but the foot position is wrong and the knees and the hips are too bent. Of course, it is always very difficult for a painter or sculptor to show movement.

A style of discus throwing based on Myron's statue, called 'the Greek style', was popular in the early Olympics at the beginning of this century. This was later discarded in favour of the modern style.

Myron's discus thrower

The Javelin

The third event of the pentathlon *Triad* was throwing the javelin. As in the long jump, the throwers had an extra aid to improve their performance: a thong held in the hand was wound round the shaft. When the javelin was released, the thong made it spin round.

Modern tests with thongs show that in most cases there is a slight increase in the distance the javelin travels.

Very little is known of the distances reached by ancient javelin throwers, but the best estimated throw is 90 metres. The present world record is 93·80 metres.

The photograph below, taken from a vase painting, shows something only found in Greek athletics. A javelin thrower, discus thrower and boxer are performing to a musical accompaniment, and we know that jumpers did this as well. The instrument is the Greek double-pipe.

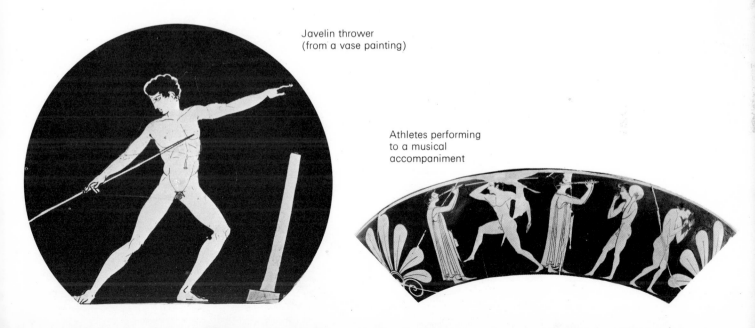

Javelin thrower
(from a vase painting)

Athletes performing
to a musical
accompaniment

Boxing

There were three 'heavy' events in Greek athletics—boxing, wrestling and a combination of the two called **pankration**. They were the most popular events, and usually had the most prize money. The same is true today; boxing and wrestling draw huge crowds at the modern Olympics, while professional boxers and wrestlers can make great sums of money.

Greek boxing was like ours in one respect: the main aim was to punch your opponent to defeat. But there were no rounds or points decisions. The boxers slugged it out till one of them was knocked out or submitted. You can see a boxer submitting in the photograph.

There were no gloves, but thongs were tied round the hands to give extra protection to the knuckles. These were called 'ants' because they stung.

Boxer submitting

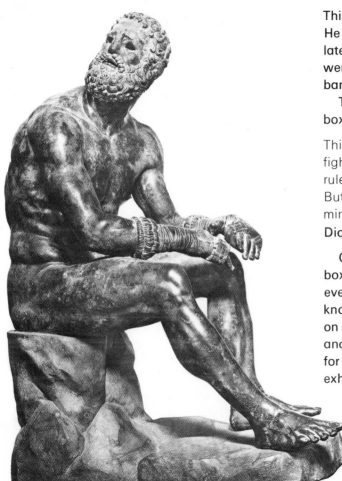

This is a famous bronze statue of an unknown Greek boxer. He is wearing the advanced type of thongs used in the later Greek games. These were carried up the forearm, and were used to wipe sweat from the forehead, like sweatbands in modern tennis.

The Greek writer Dio Chrysostom has this to say about boxing:

This is the same as in athletics, when a small man is fighting a big one. The big man is not allowed to break any rules, and is flogged, even if he breaks one accidentally. But the small one gets away with it, and no one seems to mind.
Dio Chrysostom 34.12.

Quite clearly there were no weight divisions, as in modern boxing. Very few small men could have survived in these events, because the extra weight is a great advantage. We know of only one boxer, Melancomas of Caria, who relied on skill alone. He used to wear out his opponents by dancing and skipping round them. We are told he could keep this up for two days; his opponents usually gave up through sheer exhaustion and frustration.

Bronze statue of a boxer. You can see the thongs tied round his hands to give protection to his knuckles

Wrestling

Even more popular than boxing was wrestling, because most Greeks wrestled as a hobby. The ancient equivalent of a golf club was a gymnasium, where most members wrestled. Like modern wrestling, the main aim was to get your opponent's shoulders on the ground for a count. There seems to have been no interval after each fall, and the match was decided on the best of three throws.

Before the bout, the wrestlers covered their bodies with olive oil, to keep sand and dust out of their pores. Then they applied a fine powder all over, to ensure a firm grip. After the bout, they bathed and cleaned the oily mixture off with the *strigil*, which you will remember was a blunt metal scraper used also by athletes. (Picture on page 15.)

The picture on this page shows that the throws in wrestling have not changed much since ancient times. One man has the other in a hold known in modern jargon as a 'full Nelson'.

In the following passage (the writer is unknown), an instructor is giving two boy wrestlers some very technical advice; he gives one boy the move, and the other boy the counter to that move. See if you can follow the moves.

Put your hip alongside his and grasp his head with your right. — You, throw both arms around him. — You, get under his grip. — You, push your foot between his and close with him. — You, get your right under him. — You, grip his right hand and thrust your left down on his flank. — You, push him back with your left. — You, reverse your feet and close with him. — You, counter his reverse.

Small bronze of wrestlers

The Pankration

There was another heavy event in Greek athletics which has disappeared: the *pankration*, which was a combination of boxing and wrestling. The main object was to force your opponent to submit by different holds, or knock him out.

The pankratiasts, as they were called, were allowed to kick as well as punch, as in modern Thai boxing.

The *pankration* was the most popular of the three heavy events, and often had the most prize money of all events. The explanation is simple: crowds loved the all-in action of the pankratiasts, who could punch and grapple, kick and throw.

If we are to believe the vase paintings, the umpires must have had a great deal of trouble in spotting fouls. The most common of these were biting and gouging the eye, which you can see in the photograph.

The *pankration* was widely known as the roughest and toughest of all sports. Epiktetos writes of the hardships facing the pankratiast:

He must train hard and eat little. Then in the contest he must face being gouged, sometimes dislocating a wrist or twisting an ankle, swallowing lots of sand, being flogged, and despite all this very often being defeated.
Epiktetos 3.14.14.

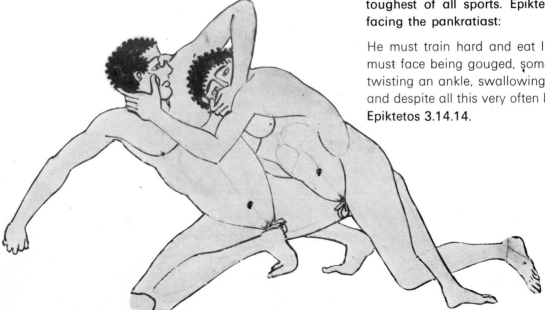

Pankratiasts gouging

Chariot Racing

The only non-athletic event in the Greek games was chariot racing; this was held on a separate track, called a **hippodrome** (race track). Not much is known of this event, as it was overshadowed by the athletics, and yet it was very popular.

The chariots were usually drawn by teams of four, six, eight or ten horses. The track was 400 metres long; it had a turning point at each end which the chariots had to go round. From the spectators' point of view, most of the excitement occurred here, as the chariots often crashed trying to make the 180° turn.

The starting line was 250 metres wide, as the number of starters could be anything up to forty. In the Pythian Games of 462 BC, there was only one chariot out of 41 that finished the course: it belonged to Arkesilaos, King of Cyrene in North Africa.

Chariot race (from a vase painting)

QUESTIONS

1 What were the four races in the Greek games? (page 18)

2 Why do you think the race in armour was not as important as some of the other events? (page 19)

3 What was a *husplex*? (page 20)

4 What were the events of the pentathlon? (page 21) What was the *Triad*?

5 What special aids were used in (**a**) the long jump (page 22) (**b**) throwing the javelin (page 27) (**c**) boxing (page 28)?

6 What sport was Phayllos famous for? What other sport did he practise? Which was his best sport? (pages 23 and 26)

7 Look at the statue of the discus thrower on page 26. What is wrong with the way the sculptor has portrayed the movement of discus throwing? (page 26).

8 What is unusual about the three athletes on page 27?

9 What difference was there between the practice jump and the real one? (page 24)

10 What constituted a false jump? (page 24)

11 How do you think music helped athletes to perform? (page 25)

12 How did wrestlers prepare for the fight? (page 30)

13 How did ancient boxing differ from modern boxing? (pages 28, 29)

14 How did the *pankration* differ from boxing and wrestling? (page 31)

15 Why was the *pankration* the most popular event of all? (page 31)

16 Why was chariot racing so dangerous? (page 32)

THINGS TO DO

1 Draw a scene at the Greek games showing EITHER the long jump OR the *pankration* OR chariot racing.

2 Find out what are the running events in the modern Olympics. Make a list of them, and compare the differences between ancient and modern.

3 What are the events of (**a**) the pentathlon (**b**) the decathlon in the modern Olympics? How was the ancient pentathlon different?

4 Imagine that you are attending the games at Olympia and see a chariot race involving a crash. Describe the scene.

5 Write a letter to the editor of the Athens Daily News complaining about a very brutal fight you have seen at Olympia. It can be *either* boxing *or* wrestling *or* the *pankration*.

4 : SOME FAMOUS ATHLETES

Milo

Milo of Croton, in Italy, was a wrestler who became a legend in his own time. He first wrestled successfully in the boys' event at Olympia in 540 BC, then he won the men's event in the next five Olympiads (the period of four years between one Olympic Games and the next), a total of twenty years. He had six victories at Delphi, ten at Corinth, and nine at Nemea. He won the quadruple crown five times, that is, he won all four 'Crown' games in the same four-year period.

Milo entered the wrestling event at Olympia for the seventh time in 516 BC, when he must have been about 40 years old. But he was beaten this time by a much younger opponent, Timasitheos, also from Croton.

Many stories were told about Milo's great strength, and some of them are hard to believe. His daily diet was 20 pounds of meat (nine kilos), 20 pounds of bread and 18 pints (six litres) of wine. On one occasion he is said to have carried a bull round the stadium at Olympia, then eaten it in one day. He used to stand on a greased discus and defy anyone to push him off it. He would hold a pomegranate uncrushed in one hand while other men exerted all their strength to prise his fingers apart. He would tie a band round his forehead and break it by swelling his veins.

The story of his death is famous. He was walking in the woods one day when he saw a tree with wedges inserted in the trunk to split it. Wishing to prove his strength had not left him, he tried to split the trunk with his bare hands. His effort was not good enough—he was trapped in the split, and unable to escape, was later attacked and devoured by a pack of wolves.

Bronze statue of wrestlers. The hold, in modern wrestling jargon, is called a 'tight waist pickup'

Theogenes

Theogenes of Thasos (an island in the Aegean Sea) had a long and distinguished career as a boxer and pankratiast. He also had a great many enemies, who were, however, unable to harm him during his lifetime.

After his death, one of them used to come at night to the public square at Thasos and flog his statue. One night the statue toppled over and crushed the man to death. The man's sons then prosecuted the statue for murder (under an ancient law this could be done). The authorities decided the best thing they could do was to get rid of the statue, so they had it dumped into the sea.

Unfortunately the crops on the island then failed, and when the Thasians sent to Delphi for advice, the oracle replied:

'You have forgotten your great Theogenes'.

The statue was fished out of the sea and set up in the Sacred Enclosure, where the Thasians from then on sacrificed to Theogenes as a god.

Wrestlers in 'head and lock' position

Pheidippides, Eukles and the Marathon

The Marathon race is one of the most famous in modern athletics, but was no part of the ancient games. The longest race was the *dolichos*, which was ten lengths at the most, or just over a mile.

The Marathon gets its name from the battle of Marathon, fought between the Greeks and Persians in 490 BC. There are two quite different versions of runs on this occasion.

The first is in the history of Herodotus, who was alive at the time of the battle. According to him, when the Persians landed at Marathon, the Athenians sent a runner, called Pheidippides, to Sparta for help. Pheidippides reached Sparta 'on the second day', that is, he covered 160 miles in less than two days, over very rough country.

This is *not* the run commemorated in the Marathon race, but was certainly the more remarkable of the two. It has been equalled since then by a South African runner called Wally Hayward, who in 1954 ran 159 miles in 24 hours non-stop, but this was on a proper track.

The more famous version of the first Marathon race is given by Plutarch, who lived in the first century AD. According to him, an Athenian called Eukles arrived late for the battle and ran all the way to Marathon. Then he fought in the battle and after it:

. . . he ran in full armour all the way to Athens hot from the battle, and bursting into the City Hall, could only say,

'Good news! We have won!' and almost at once fell down dead.

When the modern games began in 1896, it was decided to commemorate this great moment in Athens' history. And so, a race was run from Marathon to Athens, a distance of 26 miles 1100 yards. Quite fittingly, it was won by a Greek runner.

Since then the Marathon has been the most popular event in the Olympics, as it is the longest and toughest race. Since 1924, the distance has been 26 miles 385 yards, which was the length of the London Marathon in 1908.

A Mimouin, of France, who won the Marathon in 1956, running in 83 degrees of heat

1 △ Throwing the javelin (pages 21, 27)

4 △ Wrestling (pages 30, 34, 35)

2 △ Throwing the discus
(pages 21, 26, 41)

SPOT THE DIFFERENCES !

3 △ Running (page 38)

5 △ Boxing (pages 28, 29, 40, 42) Can you name the two boxers?

SOME IMPORTANT DATES

BC	c 1000	The *Iliad* and *Odyssey* are composed
	776	Foundation of Olympic Games
	540	Milo's first victory at Olympia
	490	Battle of Marathon
	146	Greece conquered by Romans
	c 50	Athletes exempt from taxes and army service
AD	c 50	Prize list from Aphrodisias
	c 100	Epiktetos and Dio Chrysostom writing
	174	Pausanias at Olympia
	396	Abolition of Games by the Emperor Theodosius
	1896	First modern Olympics in Athens

c = about

BOOKS TO READ

1 Homer's *Iliad* and *Odyssey* have accounts of athletics and are available in the Penguin Classics series. Other ancient books which mention athletics are The *Aeneid* of Virgil, the *Thebaid* of Statius, and the *Argonautica* by Apollonios.

2 Pausanias' *A Description of Greece* has a full account of Olympia (available in the Penguin Classics series).

3 M. I. Evans' *Olympic Runner* is a modern story about Greek athletics, and can be found in abridged form in *Modern Stories of Ancient Greece,* published by Longman.

4 The best account of Greek athletics is *Greek Athletes and Athletics* by H. A. Harris, available in most libraries, (published by Hutchinson).